FROM VLOGS TO VAULTS

A YouTuber's Guide to

Financial Success

By

THOMAS TELES

TABLE OF CONTENTS

Understanding YouTube as a platform

Understanding YouTube as a platform and its evolution, as well as its impact on modern media consumption.

YouTube has come a long way since its launch in 2005. Initially, it started as a platform for users to upload and share videos with others. Over time, it has evolved into a massive online community with billions of users and a wide range of content.

One of the key factors in YouTube's evolution is the rise of content creators. These individuals or groups produce videos on various topics, such as entertainment, education, beauty, gaming, and more. They have gained significant influence and have become celebrities in their own right. This shift has transformed YouTube into a platform where anyone can create and share content, democratizing the media landscape.

YouTube's impact on modern media consumption

YouTube's impact on modern media consumption is undeniable. It has revolutionized the way people consume and engage with content. Traditional media outlets, such as television and radio, have faced competition from YouTube as it offers a more personalized and interactive experience.

YouTube has also played a crucial role in the rise of online video streaming. With the introduction of YouTube Premium, users can access exclusive content, ad-free viewing, and offline playback. This has led to a shift in how people consume media, with many opting for online platforms like YouTube over traditional television.

Furthermore, YouTube has become a powerful marketing tool for businesses and brands. Many companies now utilize YouTube to reach their target audience through advertisements, sponsorship, and collaborations with popular content creators. This has opened up new opportunities for content creators to monetize their channels and make a living from their passion.

In conclusion, YouTube has evolved from a simple video-sharing platform to a global phenomenon that has transformed the way we consume media. Its impact on modern media consumption is significant, offering a diverse range of content, empowering content creators, and providing a personalized viewing experience.

YouTube's Ecosystem

Understanding YouTube as a platform involves recognizing its ecosystem, which consists of creators, viewers, and communities.

Creators are the individuals or groups who produce and upload content on YouTube. They play a vital role in shaping the platform and attracting viewers. Creators have the freedom to express their creativity and share their passions with a global audience. They can monetize their channels through various means, such as advertisements, sponsorships, and merchandise sales.

Viewers are the users who consume the content on YouTube. They have the power to choose what they want to watch and engage with the creators through likes, comments, and subscriptions. Viewers can also create playlists,

share videos with others, and discover new
content through recommendations.

Communities on YouTube are formed around
shared interests and passions. They bring together
creators and viewers who have similar
preferences and engage in discussions,
collaborations, and fan interactions. These
communities foster a sense of belonging and
provide a space for like-minded individuals to
connect and support each other.

Creators, viewers, and communities

YouTube's ecosystem thrives on the interaction
and engagement between creators, viewers, and
communities. Creators rely on viewers for their

success, while viewers rely on creators for entertaining and informative content. Communities provide a sense of belonging and facilitate connections between creators and viewers.

Overall, understanding YouTube as a platform involves recognizing the symbiotic relationship between creators, viewers, and communities. Each component plays a crucial role in shaping the YouTube ecosystem and contributing to its success.

The Psychology of YouTube Success

The psychology behind YouTube success can be quite fascinating. Successful YouTube channels often have a few key elements that contribute to their popularity. Here are some factors to consider when analyzing successful channels:

1. Consistency: Successful channels tend to have a consistent upload schedule, which helps to build a loyal audience. Regularly providing new content keeps viewers engaged and coming back for more.

2. Quality Content: The content itself plays a crucial role in a channel's success. Channels that offer unique, informative, entertaining, or inspiring content tend to attract more viewers. It's important to understand the target audience and create content that resonates with them.

3. Engagement: Successful YouTubers actively engage with their audience through comments, likes, and shares. Building a community and fostering a sense of connection with viewers can help to increase channel growth and loyalty.

4. SEO and Discoverability: Understanding search engine optimization (SEO) techniques can help channels gain visibility on YouTube. Optimizing video titles, descriptions, tags, and thumbnails can improve a channel's chances of being discovered by new viewers.

5. Collaboration: Collaborating with other successful YouTubers can help channels reach a

wider audience and gain exposure. Cross-promotion and featuring guest appearances can be mutually beneficial for both channels involved.

6. Authenticity: Viewers appreciate authenticity and genuine personalities. Successful YouTubers often showcase their true selves, allowing viewers to connect on a deeper level. Being relatable and transparent can help build trust and loyalty.

It's important to note that success on YouTube can vary greatly depending on the niche, target audience, and individual goals of the channel. Analyzing successful channels within your specific niche can provide valuable insights and

inspiration for your own YouTube journey.

Finding Your Niche and Establishing Your Brand

Finding your niche involves identifying your passion and expertise. It's important to start by self-assessing your interests and skills. Ask yourself what topics or activities you are genuinely passionate about and enjoy doing. Consider your hobbies, experiences, and any specialized knowledge you may have.

To identify your passion, think about what makes you feel excited, motivated, and fulfilled. It could be a particular subject, industry, or even a specific problem you want to solve. Reflect on what you naturally gravitate towards and what you find yourself constantly learning or talking about.

Next, assess your skills. Think about what you are good at and what comes naturally to you. Consider both hard skills (technical abilities) and soft skills (interpersonal and communication skills). Identify areas where you excel and where you can provide value to others.

Once you have a clear understanding of your passion and expertise, you can start establishing your brand. Your brand is essentially how you present yourself to the world and how others perceive you. It's important to align your brand

with your niche and showcase your unique
qualities.

To establish your brand, consider the following
steps:

1. Define your target audience: Determine who
your ideal audience or customers are. Understand
their needs, preferences, and pain points.

2. Craft your brand message: Develop a clear and
compelling message that communicates your
passion, expertise, and the value you provide.
This message should resonate with your target
audience.

3. Build your online presence: Create a
professional website or blog where you can

showcase your expertise and share valuable content. Utilize social media platforms to engage with your audience and establish yourself as an authority in your niche.

4. Network and collaborate: Connect with others in your industry or niche. Attend events, join online communities, and collaborate with like-minded individuals. Building relationships can help you expand your reach and gain credibility.

5. Consistency is key: Be consistent in your brand messaging, visual identity, and the content you produce. This helps build trust and recognition among your audience.

finding your niche and establishing your brand is an ongoing process. It may take time and experimentation to refine your focus and build a strong brand presence. Stay true to your passion and expertise, and continuously learn and adapt along the way.

Identifying Your Passion and Expertise

Finding your niche involves identifying your passion and expertise. It's important to choose a niche that aligns with your interests and skills, as this will make it easier for you to stay motivated and provide value to your audience. Start by asking yourself what topics or activities you enjoy the most and where you have the most knowledge or experience.

Once you have identified your passion and expertise, it's time to research popular niches. This involves understanding what topics or industries are currently in demand and have a large audience. You can use various tools and platforms to conduct market research, such as social media, online forums, keyword research tools, and competitor analysis.

By researching popular niches, you can gain insights into what people are interested in and what gaps exist in the market. This will help you position yourself and your brand in a unique way, offering something valuable and different from your competitors.

it's important to be authentic and genuine in your niche selection. Choose something that truly resonates with you and where you can provide value to your audience. It may take some time and experimentation to find the perfect niche, but with dedication and passion, you can establish a strong brand that stands out.

Self-assessment of interests and skills

Finding your niche involves identifying a specific target audience or market segment that you want to focus on. It's important to consider your interests, skills, and expertise when determining your niche. Ask yourself what unique value you can offer to this specific group of people. By narrowing down your focus, you can better tailor your products or services to meet the needs of your target audience.

Establishing Your Brand

Establishing your brand involves creating a strong and consistent identity that resonates with your target audience. This includes defining your Unique Value Proposition (UVP) and crafting a compelling channel identity.

Defining Your Unique Value Proposition (UVP): Your UVP is what sets you apart from your competitors and highlights the unique value you bring to your customers. It should clearly communicate the benefits and advantages of choosing your brand over others. To define your UVP, consider what problems you solve, what benefits you provide, and what makes you different from others in your industry.

Crafting a Compelling Channel Identity:
Your channel identity refers to how you present your brand across different platforms and channels, such as your website, social media, and marketing materials. It's important to maintain consistency in your branding elements, such as your logo, colors, fonts, and tone of voice. This helps to create a recognizable and memorable brand image.

Building a Consistent Brand Image:

Building a consistent brand image is crucial for establishing a strong and recognizable brand. Consistency helps to create trust and familiarity with your target audience. To build a consistent brand image, you should focus on design elements, tone, style, and messaging.

Design Elements (Logo, Banner, Thumbnails):

Design elements play a significant role in shaping your brand's visual identity. Your logo, banner, and thumbnails should reflect your brand's personality and values. It's important to create a visually appealing and professional design that resonates with your target audience. Consider using colors, fonts, and imagery that align with your brand's identity and appeal to your target market.

Tone, Style, and Messaging:

The tone, style, and messaging of your brand should be consistent across all your communication channels. This includes your website, social media, marketing materials, and customer interactions. Determine the tone and style that best represents your brand's personality and values. Whether it's formal, casual, friendly, or professional, make sure it aligns with your target audience's preferences. Additionally, your messaging should be clear, concise, and consistent, conveying your brand's unique value proposition and benefits.

By maintaining consistency in your design

elements, tone, style, and messaging, you create a

cohesive and memorable brand image that helps

differentiate you from competitors and resonates

with your target audience.

Content Creation and Production

Content creation and production are the lifeblood of any successful YouTube channel. It encompasses the entire process of conceptualizing, crafting, and delivering engaging videos to your audience. This involves brainstorming innovative ideas, honing your unique style, and utilizing the right equipment for filming and editing. Effective content creation requires a deep understanding of your target audience, allowing you to tailor your videos to their interests and preferences. It's an art that combines creativity, technical skill, and a keen eye for detail. By investing time and effort into this crucial aspect of YouTube, you set the stage for building a dedicated viewership and ultimately, a thriving channel.

Planning and Ideation

Planning and Ideation are crucial steps in ensuring the success of your YouTube channel.

1. Tutorial Videos: Create videos that teach viewers various techniques and strategies for growing their YouTube channels, such as optimizing video titles, thumbnails, and descriptions.

2. Behind-the-Scenes: Offer a glimpse into your own YouTube journey by sharing behind-the-

scenes footage of your content creation process, including planning, filming, and editing.

3. Q&A Sessions: Engage with your audience by hosting Q&A sessions where you answer their questions about YouTube success, creative potential, and monetization.

4. Case Studies: Analyze successful YouTube channels and share case studies that highlight their strategies, creative approaches, and monetization methods.

5. Collaboration Videos: Collaborate with other successful YouTubers or experts in the field to

create videos that provide valuable insights and

tips for aspiring content creators.

6. Equipment and Software Reviews: Review

different cameras, microphones, editing software,

and other equipment that can help content

creators enhance the quality of their videos.

7. Monetization Strategies: Share effective ways

to monetize a YouTube channel, such as through

ad revenue, sponsorships, merchandise, or

crowdfunding.

It's important to tailor your video ideas to your

target audience and the specific topics covered in

your book.

Brainstorming Video Ideas:

The first step in creating compelling content for your YouTube channel is brainstorming video ideas. This process involves generating a pool of potential topics, formats, and concepts that align with your channel's niche and audience interests. Here are some effective techniques to kickstart your brainstorming session:

1. Audience Feedback and Surveys: Engage with your audience through comments, social media, or surveys to gather insights into what topics they find most interesting or would like to see covered.

2. Trending Topics and News: Stay updated with current events, trends, and popular discussions within your niche. Timely content can attract a larger audience.

3. Keyword Research: Utilize tools like Google Keyword Planner, Ubersuggest, or TubeBuddy to identify high-search volume keywords related to your niche.

4. Competitor Analysis: Analyze successful channels in your niche to gain inspiration and identify content gaps that you can fill.

5. Evergreen Content: Create content that remains relevant over time. These videos can continue to attract views long after they're published.

Creating an Editorial Calendar

An editorial calendar is a crucial tool that helps you plan, organize, and schedule your content effectively. It provides structure to your content creation process and ensures a consistent flow of videos for your audience. Here's a step-by-step guide to creating an effective editorial calendar:

1. Choose a Calendar Format: You can use digital tools like Google Calendar, Trello, or specialized content management platforms like CoSchedule.

Alternatively, a physical planner or spreadsheet can work just as well.

2.Set Realistic Goals: Determine how often you want to publish videos. Start with a manageable frequency and gradually increase as you become more comfortable with your production process.

3. Identify Key Dates and Events: Note down holidays, special occasions, or industry-related events that you want to create content around. This ensures your content remains timely and relevant.

4. Assign Topics to Dates: Allocate specific video ideas to each publishing date. Make sure to

balance different types of content (e.g., tutorials, vlogs, reviews) for variety.

5. Create Production Timelines: Break down the production process for each video, including scripting, filming, editing, and any additional elements like graphics or animations.

6. Consider Batch Production: When possible, create multiple videos in one session. This can save time and ensure a consistent upload schedule.

7. Leave Room for Flexibility: While planning is essential, be open to adapting your calendar as needed. Emergencies, trends, or unexpected opportunities may arise that require adjustments.

8. Track Progress and Performance: Use analytics tools to monitor the performance of your videos. This information can help you refine your content strategy and adjust your calendar accordingly.

9. Engage with Audience Feedback: Pay attention to comments, messages, and feedback from your viewers. Use their input to refine future content ideas.

Equipment and Technical Know-How

When it comes to equipment, there are a few key components to consider. For cameras, popular options include DSLRs, mirror less cameras, and even smartphones with high-quality cameras. It's important to choose a camera that suits your needs and budget. Some popular camera brands include Canon, Nikon, Sony, and Panasonic.

For microphones, there are different types depending on your recording needs. A popular choice is a condenser microphone, which is great for capturing clear audio. USB microphones are also convenient for beginners as they can be directly connected to a computer. Some well-known microphone brands include Audio-Technical, Rode, and Blue.

Lighting is crucial for achieving professional-looking videos. You can start with basic lighting setups using affordable options like soft box lights or LED panels. It's important to have good lighting to ensure your subject is well-lit and visible.

When it comes to editing software, there are various options available. Some popular choices include Adobe Premiere Pro, Final Cut Pro, and iMovie. These software programs offer a range of features and capabilities for editing your videos.

Basic video editing techniques

As for basic video editing techniques, here are a few key concepts to keep in mind;

1. Importing and organizing footage: Start by importing your video clips into your editing software and organizing them into a logical order.

2. Cutting and trimming: Use the editing software's tools to cut and trim your clips, removing any unwanted sections or mistakes.

3. Adding transitions: Transitions can help smooth the flow between different clips. Common transitions include fades, dissolves, and cuts.

4. Adding music and sound effects: Enhance your video by adding background music or sound

effects to create a more engaging experience for your viewers.

5. Color correction and grading: Adjust the colors and tones of your footage to achieve a desired look or to correct any issues with lighting or white balance.

6. Adding text and graphics: Use text overlays and graphics to provide additional information or to enhance the visual appeal of your video.

Remember, these are just some basic techniques, and there are many more advanced techniques you can explore as you gain more experience.

Content Formats and Styles

Content formats refer to the different types of content that can be created, such as articles, videos, podcasts, infographics, and more. Each format has its own unique style and purpose. For example, articles are typically written in a more formal and informative tone, while videos can be more engaging and visual.

Tutorials:

Tutorials are a popular content format where creators provide step-by-step instructions on how to do something. They are often used to teach a specific skill or demonstrate a process. Tutorials can be created in various formats, such as written articles, videos, or even live streams.

Vlogs:

Vlogs, short for video blogs, are a type of content format where creators document their daily lives or share their experiences. Vlogs are typically more personal and casual in nature, often filmed in a diary-like style. They can be a great way to connect with your audience on a more personal level.

Reviews:

Reviews are content pieces where creators share their opinions and evaluations of products, services, or experiences. They can be in the form of written articles, videos, or even podcasts. Reviews are helpful for consumers who are looking for recommendations or insights before making a purchase.

Tailoring Content to Your Audience:

When creating content, it's important to consider your target audience and tailor your content to their preferences and interests. This involves understanding their demographics, interests, and needs. By knowing your audience, you can create content that resonates with them and provides value. This can be done by conducting audience research, engaging with your audience through comments and feedback, and analyzing data and insights from your content performance.

Audience Engagement and Community Building

Audience Engagement and Community Building:

1. What is audience engagement?

Audience engagement refers to the level of interaction and involvement that your audience has with your content or brand. It includes activities such as likes, comments, shares, and direct communication with your audience.

2. How can I increase audience engagement?

To increase audience engagement, you can:

- Create high-quality and relevant content that resonates with your target audience.

- Encourage your audience to participate by asking questions, running polls, or hosting contests.

- Respond to comments and messages promptly to show that you value their input.

- Foster a sense of community by creating a space where your audience can connect with each other.

3. What are some effective community building strategies?

Some effective community building strategies include:

- Hosting live events or webinars where your audience can interact with you and each other in real-time.

- Creating a dedicated online community or forum where your audience can discuss topics related to your brand or industry.

- Collaborating with influencers or experts in your field to provide valuable content and insights to your community.

- Recognizing and rewarding active community members to encourage participation and loyalty.

Establishing a Strong Online Presence

Establishing a Strong Online Presence is crucial for creators to connect with their audience and build a loyal community. Here are some social media strategies that can help:

1. Define your brand: Clearly define your brand identity, values, and goals. This will help you create content that aligns with your brand and resonates with your target audience.

2. Choose the right platforms: Identify the social media platforms where your target audience is most active. Focus your efforts on those platforms to maximize your reach and engagement.

3. Consistent posting schedule: Regularly post content to keep your audience engaged and interested. Consistency is key to building a strong online presence.

4. Engage with your audience: Respond to comments, messages, and mentions from your audience. Show genuine interest in their thoughts and opinions. This will help foster a sense of community and make your audience feel valued.

5. Encourage user-generated content: Encourage your audience to create and share their own content related to your brand. This can be done through contests, challenges, or simply by asking for their input and feedback.

6. Collaborate with other creators: Collaborating with other creators in your niche can help you reach a wider audience and build relationships within the community. Look for opportunities to

collaborate on content or cross-promote each
other's work.

7. Provide value: Create content that provides
value to your audience. This can be in the form of
educational content, entertainment, or inspiration.
By consistently delivering value, you will attract
and retain a loyal audience.

8. Analyze and adapt: Regularly analyze your
social media metrics to understand what content
resonates with your audience the most. Use this
data to refine your content strategy and make
improvements.

Building a strong online presence takes time and effort. Stay consistent, engage with your audience, and provide value, and you will gradually build a thriving community around your content.

Audience engagement and community building, as well as establishing a strong online presence, cross-promotion, and collaborations.

Establishing a Strong Online Presence:

1. How can I establish a strong online presence?

To establish a strong online presence, you can:

- Define your brand's unique voice and values.

- Create a consistent brand identity across all online platforms, including your website, social media profiles, and email newsletters.

- Regularly publish high-quality content that is relevant to your target audience.

- Engage with your audience through social media, blog comments, and email marketing.

- Utilize search engine optimization (SEO) techniques to improve your visibility in search engine results.

Cross-promotion and Collaborations:

1. What is cross-promotion?

Cross-promotion is a marketing strategy where two or more brands collaborate to promote each other's products or services. It allows brands to reach a wider audience and leverage each other's existing customer base.

2. How can I effectively cross-promote my brand?

To effectively cross-promote your brand, you can:

- Identify complementary brands or influencers that share a similar target audience.

- Develop mutually beneficial partnerships where you can promote each other's products or services.

- Collaborate on content creation, such as guest blogging, podcast interviews, or social media takeovers.

- Utilize social media platforms to promote your brand and engage with your audience. This can include sharing each other's content, tagging each other in posts, or running joint promotions.

- Leverage email marketing by collaborating on joint email campaigns or newsletters to reach a wider subscriber base.

- Participate in industry events or trade shows where you can network with other brands and explore cross-promotion opportunities.

- Always ensure that the partnerships you form align with your brand values and target audience to maintain authenticity and provide value to your audience.

Effective cross-promotion requires building genuine relationships and providing value to your audience.

Fostering Meaningful Connections with Your Audience

Audience engagement and community building are essential for fostering meaningful connections with your audience. It involves actively interacting with your audience, responding to their comments and messages, and creating a sense of community.

When it comes to responding to comments, it's important to acknowledge and appreciate your audience's input. Responding promptly and thoughtfully shows that you value their opinions and encourages further engagement. You can answer their questions, provide additional information, or simply thank them for their feedback.

In terms of messages, it's crucial to respond to them in a timely manner. This shows that you are attentive and interested in what your audience has to say. Whether it's through direct messages or emails, make sure to address their concerns or inquiries with sincerity and helpfulness.

Building a community involves creating a space where your audience feels comfortable and connected. Encourage discussions and interactions among your audience members by asking questions, hosting live sessions, or creating dedicated groups or forums. This helps foster a sense of belonging and encourages meaningful connections between your audience members.

authenticity is key in audience engagement and community building. Be genuine in your interactions, show empathy, and always strive to provide value to your audience. Building a strong community takes time and effort, but the rewards are worth it in terms of loyalty, trust, and long-term engagement.

Hosting live streams and Q&A sessions

Hosting live streams and Q&A sessions are great ways to foster meaningful connections with your audience and further engage with them.

Live streams allow you to interact with your audience in real-time, creating a sense of immediacy and authenticity. During live streams, you can share valuable content, answer questions, and address any concerns your audience may have. This direct interaction helps build trust and strengthens the connection between you and your audience.

Q&A sessions are another effective way to engage with your audience. By allowing them to ask questions, you demonstrate that you value their input and are willing to address their specific interests or concerns. You can host Q&A sessions through live streams, social media platforms, or even dedicated forums or groups. Encourage your audience to participate and provide them with a platform to share their thoughts and ideas.

When hosting live streams and Q&A sessions, it's important to be prepared and organized. Have a clear agenda or topic in mind, and ensure that you have the necessary equipment and technical setup to deliver a smooth experience. Interact with your audience by addressing their questions and comments, and make an effort to create a welcoming and inclusive environment.

Additionally, promoting your live streams and Q&A sessions in advance can help generate excitement and ensure a larger turnout. Use your social media platforms, email newsletters, or website to inform your audience about the upcoming event and encourage them to participate.

The key to successful audience engagement and community building is to be genuine, responsive, and provide value. By hosting live streams and Q&A sessions, you create opportunities for meaningful connections and further strengthen the bond with your audience.

Understanding YouTube Analytics

Audience engagement and community building on YouTube, as well as understanding YouTube analytics and utilizing data to refine your content strategy.

Audience engagement and community building are crucial aspects of growing and maintaining a successful YouTube channel. Here are some key points to consider:

1. Interact with your audience: Respond to comments, ask for feedback, and engage in conversations with your viewers. This helps to build a sense of community and shows that you value their input.

2. Encourage audience participation: Encourage your viewers to like, share, and subscribe to your channel. You can also ask them to leave comments or suggestions for future content. This helps to increase engagement and build a loyal community.

3. Collaborate with other creators: Collaborating with other YouTubers in your niche can help you tap into their audience and vice versa. This cross-promotion can lead to increased engagement and community growth.

YouTube analytics and tracking performance metrics

YouTube provides a wealth of analytics data that can help you understand how your videos are performing and how your audience is engaging with your content. Some important metrics to track include:

1. Views and watch time: These metrics show you how many people are watching your videos and how long they are watching for. This can help you identify which videos are resonating with your audience and which ones may need improvement.

2. Audience demographics: YouTube analytics provides insights into the age, gender, and location of your viewers. Understanding your audience demographics can help you tailor your content to better suit their interests and preferences.

3. Engagement metrics: Metrics like likes, comments, and shares indicate how engaged your

audience is with your content. Pay attention to these metrics to gauge the level of interest and interaction your videos are generating.

Utilizing data to refine your content strategy

By analyzing the data provided by YouTube analytics, you can make informed decisions to improve your content strategy. Here are some tips:

Of course! Setting specific goals and tracking your progress using analytics data can be a valuable strategy for improving your content on YouTube. Here's how you can complete that step:

1. Determine your objectives: Start by identifying what you want to achieve with your YouTube channel. Do you want to increase your subscriber count, improve watch time, or boost engagement? Set specific and measurable goals that align with your overall content strategy.

2. Use analytics data: YouTube provides various metrics and data points that can help you track your progress towards your goals. Some key metrics to consider include views, watch time, likes, comments, shares, and subscriber growth. Analyze these metrics regularly to understand how your content is performing and whether you're making progress towards your goals.

3. Set specific targets: Once you have a clear understanding of your current performance, set specific targets for each metric based on your goals. For example, if your goal is to increase watch time, you might set a target to achieve a certain number of watch hours per month.

4. Monitor and adjust: Continuously monitor your analytics data to see how you're progressing towards your targets. If you're not meeting your goals, analyze the data to identify areas for improvement. This could involve experimenting with different video formats, optimizing your titles and thumbnails, or engaging more with your audience.

5. Refine your content strategy: Based on the insights gained from your analytics data, refine your content strategy accordingly. Focus on creating more of the content that resonates with your audience and helps you achieve your goals.

Setting realistic and achievable goals is important to stay motivated and track your progress effectively. I hope this helps you complete the step of setting goals and tracking your progress using YouTube analytics!

Monetization Strategies

Monetization strategies are pivotal for achieving success on YouTube. The YouTube Partner Program (YPP) stands as a cornerstone, offering creators the opportunity to earn revenue through advertising. By meeting specific eligibility criteria and abiding by community guidelines, creators can unlock the potential for ad revenue. However, diversification is key, and savvy content creators often explore alternative revenue streams. These may encompass sponsorships, brand collaborations, merchandise sales, crowdfunding, and affiliate marketing. Each avenue presents unique opportunities to enhance earnings and establish sustainable income streams, ultimately empowering creators to continue

producing valuable and engaging content for their

audience. Balancing these strategies judiciously

can lead to a thriving and financially rewarding

YouTube channel.

YouTube Partner Program (YPP) and its monetization strategies.

The YouTube Partner Program (YPP) is a

program that allows content creators on YouTube

to monetize their videos and earn money from

their content. To be eligible for the YPP, you

need to meet certain requirements set by

YouTube. These requirements include:

1. Channel eligibility: Your channel needs to have at least 1,000 subscribers.

2. Watch time: Your channel needs to have accumulated 4,000 watch hours in the past 12 months.

3. Adherence to YouTube's policies: Your channel must comply with YouTube's Community Guidelines and Terms of Service.

Meeting these requirements is essential to be considered for the YPP. Once you meet the eligibility criteria and apply for the program, YouTube will review your channel to ensure it meets their guidelines.

Benefits of joining the YPP:

1. Monetization: The primary benefit of joining the YPP is the ability to monetize your videos. This means you can earn money through advertisements shown on your videos.

2. Access to additional features: Being a part of the YPP grants you access to various features like custom thumbnails, external annotations, and the ability to link to external websites from your videos.

3. YouTube Premium revenue: If your content is watched by YouTube Premium subscribers, you can earn a share of the revenue generated from those views.

4. Partner support: As a YPP member, you gain access to YouTube's partner support team, who

can assist you with any issues or questions you may have.

It's important to note that while joining the YPP can provide opportunities for monetization, it also comes with responsibilities. You need to adhere to YouTube's policies and guidelines to maintain your eligibility and continue earning from your content.

Advertising Revenue

Monetization strategies, specifically advertising revenue, how AdSense works, and optimizing ad placements for higher CPM.

Monetization Strategies: Advertising Revenue

Advertising revenue is a common monetization strategy used by many websites and online platforms. It involves displaying advertisements on your website or platform and earning revenue based on the number of ad impressions or clicks generated by your audience.

How AdSense Works

AdSense is a popular advertising program offered by Google. It allows website owners and publishers to display targeted ads on their websites and earn money when visitors interact with those ads. AdSense uses contextual targeting, which means that the ads displayed are relevant to the content of the website.

To use AdSense, you need to sign up for an AdSense account and get approved. Once approved, you can generate ad code from your AdSense account and place it on your website. AdSense will then automatically display relevant ads based on the content of your website and the preferences of your visitors.

Optimizing ad placements for higher CPM

Optimizing Ad Placements for Higher CPM

CPM (Cost Per Mille) refers to the amount of money advertisers are willing to pay for every thousand ad impressions. To optimize ad placements for higher CPM, you can consider the following strategies:

1. Ad Placement: Experiment with different ad placements on your website to find the most effective positions. Generally, ads placed above the fold (visible without scrolling) tend to perform better.

2. Ad Size: Test different ad sizes to see which ones generate higher CPM. AdSense offers a variety of ad sizes, so you can choose the ones that work best for your website layout.

3. Ad Formats: AdSense offers various ad formats, including text ads, display ads, and native ads. Experiment with different formats to see which ones attract higher CPM rates.

4. Ad Relevance: Ensure that the ads displayed on your website are relevant to your content and audience. This increases the chances of visitors engaging with the ads, leading to higher CPM rates.

5. Ad Blocking: Monitor your website for ad-blocking software and take steps to minimize its impact. Ad-blocking can significantly reduce your ad impressions and revenue.

Optimizing Ad placements for higher CPM requires continuous testing and experimentation. It's important to analyze your ad performance regularly and make adjustments accordingly.

Alternative Revenue Streams

Monetization strategies and alternative revenue streams. Here are some common methods:

1. Sponsorships and brand deals: Many content creators collaborate with brands to promote their products or services. This can involve sponsored content, product placements, or brand partnerships. Creators receive compensation in exchange for promoting the brand to their audience.

2. Merchandise: Selling merchandise, such as clothing, accessories, or other branded items, can be a great way to generate revenue. Content

creators often design and sell their own merchandise, leveraging their brand and fanbase.

3. Crowdfunding: Crowdfunding platforms like Patreon or Kickstarter allow creators to receive financial support directly from their audience. Creators can offer exclusive content, early access, or other perks to their supporters in exchange for their contributions.

4. Affiliate marketing: Content creators can earn a commission by promoting products or services through affiliate links. When their audience makes a purchase using the provided link, the creator receives a percentage of the sale.

These are just a few examples of alternative revenue streams for content creators. It's important to note that the effectiveness of each strategy can vary depending on factors such as audience size, niche, and engagement levels.

Legal and Copyright Considerations

Legal and copyright considerations are paramount for achieving success on YouTube. Understanding and adhering to copyright laws ensures that you're using content responsibly and within legal boundaries. This includes obtaining licenses or permissions for any copyrighted material you don't own. Additionally, protecting your intellectual property through trademarks and copyrights safeguards your original content from unauthorized use. It's essential to also familiarize yourself with YouTube's Community Guidelines and Policies to avoid content that may lead to demonetization or channel strikes. By respecting legal and copyright principles, you not only maintain a trustworthy reputation but also safeguard your channel's long-term viability and potential for growth.

You can consider the following:

1. Understanding Copyright Laws: Copyright laws protect original works of authorship,

including text, images, videos, and music. As a

content creator, it's important to understand these

laws to avoid infringing on someone else

copyright. Generally, copyright protection lasts

for the creator's lifetime plus a certain number of

years.

2. Fair Use and Public Domain: Fair use is a legal

doctrine that allows limited use of copyrighted

material without permission from the copyright

owner. This includes purposes such as criticism,

commentary, news reporting, teaching, and

research. Public domain refers to works that are

not protected by copyright and can be freely used

by anyone.

3. Obtaining Licenses and Permissions: If you want to use copyrighted material in your content, it's best to obtain proper licenses or permissions from the copyright owner. This can involve contacting the copyright holder directly or using licensing platforms that provide access to a wide range of content.

It's important to note that copyright laws can vary between countries, so it's advisable to consult with a legal professional or refer to the specific laws in your jurisdiction. Understanding and respecting copyright laws will help you avoid legal issues and protect your own intellectual property.

Protecting Your Intellectual Property

Legal and copyright considerations related to protecting your intellectual property, including trademarks, copyrights, and patents.

Trademarks are used to protect brand names, logos, and slogans that distinguish goods or services in the marketplace. Registering a trademark with the appropriate government agency can provide legal protection and prevent others from using similar marks that may cause confusion among consumers.

Copyrights, on the other hand, protect original works of authorship such as literary, artistic, musical, or dramatic creations. This includes books, songs, paintings, photographs, and software. Copyright protection is automatic upon creation, but registering your copyright with the relevant copyright office can provide additional legal benefits, such as the ability to sue for infringement.

Patents protect inventions and grant exclusive rights to the inventor for a limited period of time. In order to obtain a patent, the invention must be novel, non-obvious, and have utility. Patents can be granted for various types of inventions, including processes, machines, compositions of matter, and designs.

To protect your intellectual property, it is important to take certain steps. First, conduct a thorough search to ensure that your idea or creation is not already protected by someone else's trademark, copyright, or patent. If it is, you may need to modify your idea or seek permission from the rights holder.

If your intellectual property is original and not already protected, you can consider registering for trademark, copyright, or patent protection. This will provide you with legal rights and remedies in case of infringement.

Additionally, it is important to use proper notices, such as the copyright symbol (©), trademark symbol (™), or registered trademark symbol (®), to indicate your ownership of intellectual property. This can help deter potential infringers and provide evidence of your rights.

It is also advisable to keep records of your creation process, including dates, sketches, drafts, and any other evidence of your work. This can be useful in case of disputes or challenges to your ownership.

Lastly, it is important to regularly monitor and enforce your intellectual property rights. This may involve sending cease and desist letters to infringers, taking legal action if necessary, or licensing your intellectual property to others for a fee.

Dealing with copyright claims and disputes

Legal and copyright considerations, as well as how to protect your intellectual property and deal with copyright claims and disputes.

When it comes to protecting your intellectual property, there are a few key steps you can take. First and foremost, it's important to understand that copyright protection automatically applies to original works of authorship, such as writings, music, art, and software, as soon as they are created and fixed in a tangible form. However, registering your copyright with the appropriate government agency, such as the United States Copyright Office, can provide additional benefits and legal protections.

To protect your intellectual property, you should consider the following:

1. Copyright Notices: Including a copyright notice on your work can help deter potential infringers and make it clear that you are the owner of the copyright. A copyright notice typically consists of the copyright symbol (©), the year of first publication, and the name of the copyright owner.

2. Licensing: If you want to allow others to use your work while still retaining control over it, you can consider licensing your intellectual property. This allows you to set specific terms and conditions for others to use your work, while still maintaining your rights as the copyright owner.

3. Trademarks: If you have a unique brand name, logo, or slogan associated with your intellectual property, you may want to consider registering it as a trademark. Trademarks provide legal protection for your brand and can help prevent others from using similar marks that could cause confusion among consumers.

Dealing with copyright claims and disputes. If you believe someone has infringed upon your copyright, you have several options:

1. Contact the Infringer: Start by reaching out to the person or entity you believe has infringed upon your copyright. Explain your concerns and provide evidence of your ownership. In some cases, this may be enough to resolve the issue amicably.

2. Cease and Desist Letter: If contacting the infringer directly doesn't resolve the issue, you can send a cease and desist letter. This formal letter demands that the infringer immediately stop

using your copyrighted material and may include a request for compensation or damages.

3. Legal Action: If all else fails, you may need to pursue legal action. Consult with an intellectual property attorney who can guide you through the process of filing a lawsuit and seeking remedies for copyright infringement.

legal and copyright considerations when it comes to YouTube's Community Guidelines and Policies, content restrictions and prohibited activities, and avoiding demonetization and channel strikes.

Adhering to YouTube's Community Guidelines and Policies

Adhering to YouTube's Community Guidelines and Policies is crucial to maintaining a successful and compliant channel. These guidelines cover various aspects such as hate speech, harassment, violence, nudity, and copyright infringement. It's important to familiarize yourself with these guidelines to ensure your content meets the platform's standards.

When it comes to copyright considerations, it's essential to respect the intellectual property rights of others. Using copyrighted material without permission can lead to copyright strikes, which may result in penalties or even the termination of your channel. To avoid copyright issues, you can either create your own original content or use content that is licensed under Creative Commons or in the public domain.

Content restrictions and prohibited activities on YouTube include but are not limited to explicit or adult content, harmful or dangerous acts, misleading information, and scams. Violating these restrictions can lead to demonetization or even the removal of your channel. It's important to review and understand these restrictions to ensure your content complies with them.

To avoid demonetization and channel strikes, it's crucial to follow YouTube's policies and guidelines. This includes avoiding copyright infringement, adhering to content restrictions, and being mindful of the community's standards. Additionally, regularly reviewing and updating your content to ensure it aligns with YouTube's policies can help maintain a monetized channel and avoid penalties.

It's always a good idea to consult YouTube's official documentation and seek legal advice if you have specific concerns or questions regarding legal and copyright considerations on the platform.

Conclusion

In the dynamic world of YouTube, success is not solely measured in subscribers and views, but also in the fulfillment derived from sharing one's creativity and expertise. By embracing the principles outlined in this guide, aspiring creators can unlock their full potential and build thriving channels that resonate with audiences around the globe. Remember, true success on YouTube is a journey of continuous learning, innovation, and authentic engagement.

YouTube Goldmine: Unleashing Your Creative Potential and Monetizing Your Channel is a game-changing guide that will empower you to take your YouTube journey to new heights. Packed with powerful strategies, practical tips, and insider secrets, this book is your ultimate road map to achieving success on the world's largest video-sharing platform.

In this book, you will discover how to tap into your creative potential and unleash your unique voice to captivate and engage your audience. Whether you're a beginner or an experienced YouTuber, you'll find valuable insights on content creation, video production, and storytelling techniques that will set you apart from the competition.

But it doesn't stop there. YouTube Success goes
beyond just creating great content. It delves into
the art of building a loyal community, fostering
meaningful connections with your viewers, and
leveraging the platform's algorithms to maximize
your reach. You'll learn how to optimize your
videos for search, create eye-catching thumbnails,
and craft compelling titles and descriptions that
will attract more viewers to your channel.

Monetization is a key aspect of YouTube success,
and this book leaves no stone unturned in guiding
you through the various revenue streams
available. From advertising and sponsorships to
merchandise and crowdfunding, you'll gain a

deep understanding of how to monetize your channel effectively and sustainably.

But what truly sets this book apart is its emphasis on authenticity and passion. YouTube Success encourages you to stay true to yourself and your vision, reminding you that success is not just about numbers but about making a genuine impact on your audience. You'll find inspiring stories from successful YouTubers who have turned their passion into a thriving career, proving that with dedication and perseverance, anything is possible.

So, if you're ready to unlock your creative potential, build a thriving YouTube channel, and turn your passion into profit, YouTube Success: Unleashing Your Creative Potential and Monetizing Your Channel is the ultimate guide you've been waiting for. Get ready to embark on an exciting journey that will transform your YouTube dreams into reality.

www.ingramcontent.com/pod-product-compliance
Lightning Source LLC
Chambersburg PA
CBHW062349290526
45794CB00005B/2150